Pretty Eyes Pastor

Pretty Eyes Pastor
Clergy Sexual Abuse
EFT Tapping

Tiffany Denmark

J. Irwin Press

Published by:
❋
J. Irwin Press
Chicago, Illinois

First Edition © 2013 by Tiffany Denmark

Paperback ISBN: 978-0-9911634-1-0
Ebook ISBN: 978-0-9911634-2-7

All rights reserved. No part of this publication may be reproduced, stored in a retrieval system, or transmitted in any form or by any means, electronic, mechanical, photocopying, recording, scanning, or otherwise, except as permitted under Sections 107 or 108 of the 1976 United States Copyright Act, without either the prior written permission of the publisher, or authorization through payment of the appropriate per-copy fee. Requests for permission should be addressed clientservices@wordsharp.net.

Contents

Dedication v

Acknowledgements vi

Key Discussion Points vii

Chapter 1: Lured Into Abuse 1

Chapter 2: Seeds Of Shame 7

Chapter 3: Emotional Destruction 27

Chapter 4: Damage From Church Politics 41

Chapter 5: The Road To Recovery With EFT 62

Adult Survivor Profile 77

Sexual Abuse Websites 78

References 80

Dedication

This book was written in dedication to the adult immigrant survivor who shared her experience of childhood abuse with me. She bore a child fathered by the family pastor when she was only twelve years old but because of a fear of deportation, her family never reported the abuse. By the time she was an adult with sufficient moral and financial support to seek legal recourse the statute of limitations had expired. After hearing this, I was inspired to use my experience of clergy childhood sexual abuse in the Baptist church as a tool to advocate on behalf of silent victims. To the memory of all sexual abuse victims who were not able to overcome their emotional grief and felt that committing suicide was their only route of escape to freedom, may they rest in peace.

Acknowledgements

I would like to thank Lyn Schollett and Polly Poskin from the Illinois Coalition Against Sexual Assault (ICASA) for giving me the opportunity to share my experience during a legislative process and for all of their kindhearted support.

In addition, I must give a special thank you to Attorney Marc Pearlman for directing me down a path of advocacy that allowed my voice to have significance.

Key Discussion Points On Story Facts

GENERAL DISCUSSION POINTS
* **Proper use of Forgiveness:**
  Controlled forgiveness with conditions
  Emotional forgiveness without conditions
  (often induced from spiritual guilt)

* **Proper use of:**
  Spiritual Governance in life
  Legal Governance in life

PSYCHOLOGY/SOCIOLOGY DISCUSSION POINTS
* Different emotional effects with clergy sexual abuse verses family molestation, assault by strangers, etc.
* Difference between silence, privacy and secrecy
* Methods used to shame victim
* Methods used to lure victim
* Post trauma effects

RELIGIOUS DISCUSSION POINTS
* Clergy brotherhood code of silence
* Violations of ministerial ethics
* Abuse of power
* Spiritual abuse
* Betrayal of trust
* Church politics

LEGAL DISCUSSION POINTS
* Violation of public trust
* Violation of public safety (child safety)
* Church liability (in-state and out-of-state)

* Criminal or civil evidence useful for other abuse cases
* Criminal or civil violations other than child sexual abuse
* Litigation limitations for religious institutions versus schools and other organizations where state regulation establishes minimum standards for employees that have direct contact with children

ALTERNATIVE THERAPY DISCUSSION POINTS

* **EFT assisted with resolving or decreasing:**
  Hopelessness
  Resentment
  Depression
  Anger
  Fear

REPORT

CLERGY CHILD SEXUAL ABUSE

TO THE POLICE

NOT

THE CHURCH

CALL 911

PERSONNEL LEGALLY QUALIFIED TO EVALUATE CHILD (minor) SEXUAL ABUSE WILL DETERMINE IF THE ALLEGATIONS HAVE MERIT

What Is Child (or minor) Sexual Abuse?

At the extreme end of the spectrum, sexual abuse includes sexual intercourse or its deviations. Yet all offences that involve sexually touching a child, as well as non-touching offenses and sexual exploitation, are just as harmful and devastating to a child's well-being.

Touching sexual offenses include:
- fondling,
- making a child touch an adult's sexual organs or
- penetrating a child's vagina or anus no matter how slight with a penis or any object that doesn't have a valid medical purpose.

Non-touching sexual offenses include:
- engaging in indecent exposure or exhibitionism,
- exposing children to pornographic material,
- deliberately exposing a child to the act of sexual intercourse or
- masturbating in front of a child.

Sexual exploitation can include:
- engaging a child or soliciting a child for the purposes of prostitution or
- using a child to film, photograph or model pornography.

The response from the child (minor):

Even a child (a minor) who does not understand

they are being harmed at the time of the abuse can exhibit negative emotional and physical effects later in life.

Be aware that it is common for those who experience childhood (a minor) sexual abuse to have a very strong emotional attachment to their abuser and may even have a desire to protect them and not demonstrate any fear.

Common signs of abuse:
- unexplained injuries,
- changes in behavior,
- fear of going home or with a particular person,
- change in sleeping habits,
- changes in performance at school,
- inappropriate sexual behavior or play acting out gestures and
- please listen and believe until definitively proved otherwise when a child (minor) says they are being touched or are engaging in an inappropriate relationship with an adult.

PRAY FOR

A

VICTIM/SURVIVOR

CHAPTER ONE

LURED INTO ABUSE

Sometimes, the beginning of child sex abuse starts with the abuser finding an emotional path to lure the child

The Sunday evening service ended late at night on the first day of a weeklong revival. The guest preacher had delivered a dynamic message with a catchy sermon title named after one of the latest TV commercial jingles. People had been dancing with joy all over the church. The congregation showed their appreciation for hearing a good sermon financially. When the offering plate was passed around, the ushers had to put their hand on top of the money to hold it down because the bills were piled up high.

The guest preacher was a friend of my family and a former member of the church who had left to accept a pastoral position a few years earlier. My parents had important business to discuss with other adults in the church basement and they were not ready to leave after the service was over. I was tired and wanted to get some sleep. The guest pastor offered to give me a ride home. Since he was a friend of the family that seemed to be a kind gesture.

Being an only child, I was what they called a latchkey child who was responsible enough to be home alone when my parents were working. I wore a key to the house strung on a ribbon or a shoestring tied around my neck hidden inside my shirt. Before leaving the church, we stopped in a room where the guest pastor changed his socks and shoes. Playfully, he lifted the front of my dress and said my legs were pretty. We both smiled with laughter in between the two kisses he gave me on the lips.

There was a wonderful smell in the guest pastor's big beautiful car coming from the pine tree scented air freshener that was hanging from the rearview mirror, until he lit a cigarette and smoke started blowing around. I just sat quietly in the comfortable crushed velvet seats. I was so short my feet did not even touch the floor.

I should have gotten right out of the car and gone directly into the house. The one night that I decided to take a journey on what I thought would be an exciting adventure for just a temporary moment in time turned out to be a decision that changed my life forever.

It was raining when he parked in front of the house. The streetlights were out from the thunderstorm and the block was completely dark while the heavy rain obscured the view from the car windows. The guest pastor put his hand on my thigh. That made me smile because I liked him just as everyone else did at the church.

Tiffany Denmark

In the past, when I came out of the bathroom at church, sometimes we were the only two people in the basement where he often went to smoke a cigarette during service. In a playful manner, he hugged me, kissed on me, rubbed my thighs, pulled me in close touching his groin area, pulled on my panties and gently patted me on the butt. It was all just fun and games to me. Unknowing, he was grooming me to become comfortable enough to trust him.

After taking off his tinted eyeglasses, I saw his eyes for the first time.

Breathless, staring from being taken by surprise, I told him that he had the prettiest eyes I had ever seen on a man. The color was so beautiful; the direction of the moonlight shining through the rain glare on the window seemed to make them sparkle. Admiring their beauty completely captured my attention for a moment. He always wore eyeglasses or shades to shield the brightness from hurting his light colored eyes and to prevent the women at church from gathering around adoring them and giving him compliments.

At first, I did not even notice that his hand was now under my dress with a finger touching my innocence as he kept looking at me with tears filling his pretty eyes while telling me there were many things happening in his life that were difficult to understand. Although he could make others happy at church, he felt very sad inside of his heart.

Concerned with his sadness, after I saw a tear roll down his face, I immediately told him not to cry. My heart became heavy from the weight of his emotions. I almost started to cry after seeing tears coming from such pretty eyes or from the slow somber gospel music playing that always made everyone cry at church funerals. He asked me if I would give him a kiss and I did. Then he asked me if I had a boyfriend and I told him that I did not.

He was long time clergy friends with my father and knew I would be twelve years old soon. To validate my level of maturity, he began telling me the mother of Jesus was only twelve years old, which shows that age is old enough for a girl to have a relationship with a grown man. He said that children kept secrets but adults kept matters confidential and I was mature enough to be in a confidential situation. Evaluating my willingness to be lured into his pedophilic lust trap, he asked me if I wanted to be his girlfriend. Naively curious, I said yes.

A grown man had never asked me that question before so I did not know exactly what he was asking me, because young relationships and sex were never discussed when I was in school, at church, at home or any place that I remember.

Adults always requested that children leave the room when they were talking. My common knowledge was limited, but I knew that a grown man did not want a girlfriend just to have someone he could play a game of marbles with or to push on the swing in the park even though I was the highest swinger on the block.

My knowledge of sex consisted of gathering around the fence with my friends watching two dogs humping on each other in the yard. We knew something mannish was occurring because an adult would always make us stop looking, but we did not understand exactly what we were watching.

In the past, children could not participate in activities or even wear clothes that were not considered age appropriate by adults. When our parents took us shopping for Sunday clothes, often they would ask for the opinion of another parent in the store and refused to even buy a pair of shoes that might look too grown up.

Since children were shielded from the adult world so much back then, anytime we became privy to learn about something out of our limited realm, it always seemed to be very exciting and intriguing. When Pretty Eyes Preacher asked me if I wanted to learn what I needed to know so I could be his girlfriend, naively eager, I said yes!

I was too young to have known that making a connection with one man on one night would be an experience that would merge into my emotions during the developmental years of my life and become a subtle influence in my mind misdirecting my heart for many years into the future. I eventually learned that the effects of the choices made by a young person could last much longer than just for a brief moment in time.

CHAPTER TWO

SEEDS OF SHAME

Sometimes, after an abuser has lured a child down a path of destruction, they often cause them to remain there by planting thoughts of fear or shame in their mind

Pretty Eyes Pastor put a tape in the player, then reached into the glove box and took out a small magazine from inside a zipped Bible cover. He took a bottle out of his travel bag, filled a plastic cup with wine, and pressed the cup on my lips telling me to drink. The grape taste was slightly bitter but it was sweet enough that I did not mind drinking while he flipped through the pages of the magazine. It was common for ministers to visit and serve communion to members at their home. Back then, it was common for them to carry the wine in their car. If the police had pulled beside the car, he would not have any acceptable excuse for giving a minor some type of liquor such as vodka. However, a member of the clergy giving the common brand of wine used for church communion could skillfully manipulate an explanation around the law.

Excited to be in the presence of a man who so many other women loved, I did not even consider why he was giving me this drink when it was not the first Sunday. After asking me to be his girlfriend, I had a sense of feeling special just as when the most popular boy in class walked me home after school one day.

I was about to become engaged in sexual encounters that I did not fully understand. They would cause me to live in secrecy, shame and fear.

When he showed me one of the pages, it was a picture of a woman firmly holding a man's phallus with an outflowing of his love running down her hand. I immediately felt confused and curious as he raised my hand putting the cup to my lips silently encouraging me to drink more. I thought it was all right drinking what I knew to be the same thing I was given at church during first Sunday communion, but I had never drank more than about a tablespoon before. I do not think I understood the effects of the alcohol because it was so sweet tasting. The preachers in church always said the Holy Ghost made people laugh for no reason, feel lightheaded and sometimes they passed out drunk in the spirit.

He said it was time for me to become a mature young woman and increase the level of my knowledge and experience above any other young woman who was in my age group. The explanation for what I saw on the woman's hand in the magazine was that it showed an outward display of how men let women know they loved them and if nothing comes out then the woman had not made the man love her. Every mature young woman did whatever was required of her to see this outward response if she wanted a man to fall in love with her.

He intensely focused his pretty eyes on me while saying I could make him happy enough that he would never cry again if I could show him that I was mature enough to make him love me. While he looked at me, his words seemed sincere and heartfelt causing me to become overwhelmed with emotion. His eyes were so pretty that they seemed to pierce through me and touch my heart. The somber music, wine, and cigarette smoke were causing me to have a warm sensation all over my body that I had never felt before. Never having these feelings before, I allowed him to direct my ignorant desire to make him happy and love me after he drew me in emotionally.

I did not realize that he was a man with the ability to perform greatly on demand in the pulpit and arouse emotional responses from adults even if he was not being sincere. My young heart was not strong or mature enough even to develop a plan to protect itself from this type of influential power.

Reaching inside his suit jacket, he took a handkerchief out of his pocket and laid it across his thigh. His strong hand grabbed mine placing it inside his pants with his hand on top of mine guiding me. Then, when he let go, I continued to move in the up and down motion as he instructed in a whispering voice while he continued to look at me with his pretty eyes commanding my attention to be on the unspoken language coming from his eyes. A few minutes later, he gave a gentle sigh. When I felt wetness on my hand, he told me that I had made him love me. As I sat there trying to understand exactly what happened, he wiped my hand clean with the handkerchief. I asked if he was wiping off the same thing that I had seen in the picture. When he smiled and said yes, I smiled within myself for being mature enough to make him happy.

Most of the men in the clergy brotherhood back then were also members of the Masonic Lodge; they exclude the outside world from sacred secrets known only by them. My image of Pretty Eyes Pastor, the sacred music-playing, communion wine, his reference to the mother of Jesus being my age and the captivating beauty of his eyes caused me to believe that by allowing me to participate in this confidential act of so-called love he was engaging me in a secret sacred experience. Obviously, he possessed something greater than the average person for everyone in the church and neighborhood to seek out his divine power. If he were just one of our friendly non-church-going neighbors playing secular music and attempting to trick me into drinking whiskey or luring me with things that were not familiar, then I would have immediately resisted.

Pretty Eyes Pastor made sure that I understood the rules of being in a confidential relationship now that I was his girlfriend. I could only speak to him and keep walking. I could not sit at the table next to him while we were eating in the church basement and most importantly, I was only to look his way when he was preaching and everyone else was looking at him. It was a great advantage that I was an only child with a quiet personality because he knew that I did not talk excessively, his greatest joy seemed to be in knowing that my monthly menstrual cycles had not begun. Each time he lovingly commended me for complying with his rules, I felt proud of my matureness.

I felt dizzy and slightly stumbled after getting out of the car. Pretty Eyes Pastor walked me to the front door with his arm around me. After giving me a kiss on the lips, he told me to go straight to bed, which I did. I laid down wondering why one of the women who were always prancing around in front of him at church did not put their hand inside his pants and make him fall in love and why he always seemed to find some excuse to avoid being around his wife when she came to town with him. He told me they had slept in separate rooms for many years and when I became older, I would understand that he was doing that because he loved me.

It was going to be a while before Pretty Eyes Pastor would visit again. Because of a lack of understanding concerning adult relationships, a number of issues left me confused. He became annoyed with me after asking him too many questions about his wife and other women around the church. We were talking in the church kitchen when he became very upset forcefully picking me up, then straddling me across his lap while talking with a cigarette in his mouth. He told me the only reason he would not stand in the pulpit and tell everyone about what I had done with him was because of his love for me and he did not want me to be an embarrassment to my family. So I apologized for making him angry, then I began crying and thanking him for being concerned about me.

Pretty Eyes Pastor was a friend of the family through my father who was an associate minister who was being referred to preach at different vacant churches possibly to obtain a pastoral position. He was a prominent pastor in the Baptist denomination and had given my father recommendations. Any scandal involving his daughter would have destroyed many of the opportunities he was being offered. My mother always sung a solo during his visits, at his request; he loved to hear the sound of her voice.

The double standards were very strong in the church at that time, when a teen girl or an unmarried woman became pregnant they were not allowed to participate in any auxiliaries at the church, but the boys and men were never reprimanded for sinful behavior.

Pretty Eyes Pastor let me know his intentions of teaching me different ways to make him happy before he left town. Though I was unaware of the actions he would take or how I would react to them, the threat of being publically embarrassed at church overpowered any feelings of fear. In the church, personal opinion held greater importance than facts.

Only my parents and I lived in our home, but we had six bedrooms and three bathrooms. On the last day of revival, my parents gave me a set of clean sheets and towels to prepare the upstairs guest room for Pretty Eyes Pastor. He checked out of the hotel that morning and was going to rest at our home during the day. After the night service he was leaving town.

When he arrived, my father had already left for a business meeting that I knew would last all day and midafternoon my mother left for her part-time job. I had to stay around the house in case he needed anything or to unlock the house door if he needed to leave out.

The phone rang on our second line; it was Pretty Eyes Pastor asking me to bring an ashtray upstairs. He was sitting in the recliner naked smoking a cigarette while watching television after taking a shower.

I had never seen a naked man before in my life. The night we were in the car, he told me to keep looking into his eyes; I did as he asked. His pretty eyes demanded that my attention remain on them the entire time. Thinking back to a conversation I overheard my grandmother having with her friends, they said all sexual acts were always performed discretely in the dark, and that led me to believe that even my mother had never seen my father naked with the lights on before. I thought I was experiencing a revelation that even few adult women had seen. Although I was afraid at the same time for a brief moment, I felt a sense of being special to have this shared with me. He was careful to let my responses direct the path he could take to prey on me then safely escape.

When I gave him the ashtray, there were four glasses sitting on the table filled with wine from a bottle that was the common brand name used at the church for communion, he gave me a straw and made a game out of drinking quickly. I really liked him and did not mind playing along as he smiled and laughed with me. Then he filled the glasses repeatedly and we drank quickly until I became intoxicated. There was another bottle that he had already been drinking but did not share any of the stronger alcohol with me. I kept looking at the hair that was all over his body; curious about the texture, I began rubbing his chest and stomach. He was just sitting there quietly smoking a cigarette watching me with a sly smile while I explored his body; his manipulation was always lowered down to a subtle level that would not intimidate me.

Then he leaned back in the chair exposing his full nakedness. Suddenly, I stood still, just holding my hands together curiously looking at the full view of his firm intension directed toward me while he pressed another glass of grape-tasting wine on my lips. If I had seen pictures of naked men before, I do not believe his body would have been as intriguing. It was just a reflection of the typical sweet potato pie eating moderate potbelly preacher.

After drinking, he kissed me about six times; then I just stood there not knowing what to say or do. Pretty Eyes Pastor kept looking at me slightly smiling and kissing me while taking off my pretty yellow sundress and matching panties. I became afraid, and through my tears, kept looking at his eyes as much as I could as he requested. The wine and the somber music playing eventually did seem to make me feel calm.

When he laid me on the couch, I was extremely dizzy while he was kissing me on my innocence. I kept wondering and wanted to ask him why he was kissing me down there, but my lightweight floating thoughts seemed to prevent me from forming the words and speaking. I heard him make a reference to enjoying a pure fresh scent that could never be found with adult women. When he rose up to look at me, my vision appeared to have become overly enhanced. It seemed that the color in his eyes had become even more beautiful. He told me to keep looking at them. Their magnetic attraction would not allow me to look away even though I was feeling

piercing discomfort from the repeated attempts to enter fully. I wanted to cry out with each teardrop, but the authority speaking to me through his eyes demanded my attention while silently entering through the weakly structured gateway of my heart leaving me laying there helpless, just staring. Then, I was suddenly stunned; seeing the outflow of his so-called love on my body made me upset. I began crying from confusion wondering why he put that wetness all over me. I did not understand its meaning. Disgruntled, I just wanted him to clean it off me.
Holding me in his arms, wiping me off with a damp towel while telling me that he only wanted to show me love outwardly did not console me, I kept crying. He reminded me of the picture he showed me in the car and tried to reassure me that I had done something wonderful for him, but I kept crying.

He lit a cigarette, then began gently blowing smoke into my eyes and nostrils until my eyelids became heavy. In a very soft compassionate voice, he started singing the song "yes Jesus loves me for the Bible tells me so." Hearing the words I had heard many times before in the safety and security of the church made me feel a familiar sense of comfort as I drifted off to sleep. I woke up later fully dressed lying across the bed downstairs in my room. He was upstairs studying the Bible to prepare his sermon for the night service, concealing his disgraceful activity with piety when my parents arrived home.

That night, I stayed in the bed suffering from a bad headache and vomiting. There was a large bag of cookies on my dresser and my parents scorned me assuming that I had overeaten until I became sick, as I had done before. They asked the neighbor to check on me while they were at church. I was happy and sad when Pretty Eyes Pastor finally left, knowing it would be a few months before I had to let him touch me again to keep him from telling anyone about our involvement gave me a little peace of mind. However, I felt a slight longing to learn the different silent commands given by his pretty eyes as I wondered if I would ever encounter this situation again.

The next month on the first Sunday, when the tray of communion cups were passed around at church, I picked up one and held it waiting to drink when the smell of the wine made me nauseous. I held my head down afraid to look around. The imagined thoughts in my mind caused me to believe that everyone in the church was looking at me and they all knew I had been drinking this same wine getting drunk with Pretty Eyes Pastor. As soon as the cup touched my lips, I began to vomit. I was extremely embarrassed; a relative escorted me to the bathroom. For several months after that incident, I sat in the church basement while communion was being served, fearing I would begin vomiting in the sanctuary in front of everyone again.

Pretty Eyes Pastor called sometimes on Thursday

evenings when my mother was at choir rehearsal and my father bowled with his league. I always stayed home with a few of my older cousins who always came over to visit. Once, my father was home and answered the phone; Pretty Eyes Pastor just carried on a conversation as though he were calling to speak with him.

Of course, pedophiles always have friends and one of his was an associate minister assigned to oversee the prayer line for a church that had a Sunday radio broadcast that came on the air in Chicago. When my family discovered that I was talking to his friend during the week after connecting with him on the prayer line, as Pretty Eyes Pastor had instructed me to do, there was a negative reaction and I could not reveal the truth of how I connected to him. From the demeanor of his voice, I thought he was a pervert who seemed to be seeking a young girl to prey upon himself. He asked me detailed questions about the type of panties I saw my little girlfriends wearing when we changed clothes in the locker room for gym class and spoke of coming by the church to visit.
My father was such a sociable kindhearted man that he would have welcomed him into his circle of clergy friends who often came to visit at our home. After that negative situation subsided, I could never say anything to an adult that would have made his friend appear to be a pedophile or I would have really been in trouble. I never spoke another word about any information I had related to clergy pedophiles.

In hindsight, it didn't make sense for Pretty Eyes Pastor to have me connect with his pedophile friend unless he believed that if my sexual abuse were discovered there would be another person in the equation to divert the attention away from any accusation made about him. I was always home on Thursday evenings but after the incident with his friend, he never called me again.

I grew up during the time when children were to be seen and not heard. Adults were very confident that if a child spoke against them it would result in the child being slapped across the mouth. The standard belief that a child's voice was insignificant enabled many adults to take advantage of children. Then, when a child waits until they are an adult to reveal the truth, they are punished by family and the legal system for failing to make the abuse known when they were a child, causing them to feel powerless to victimization twice.

I felt powerless against adults as a child. Later, I lacked the power to overcome adverse situations that occurred in most of my adult life. The calls from Pretty Eyes Pastor appeared to be out of concern for me, his girlfriend, but they were really to verify that I had been quiet about our involvement and to subtly reinforce my fear of the consequences if I revealed our sacred confidence and told anyone that I had let him take off my panties. When I became an adult that subtle mental intimidation transformed into fear of rumors, judgments and stereotyping that could affect my personal life. It was simply a grown up version of my childhood fear of being whipped and punished for my actions.

My father had numerous preacher friends who visited our home on a regular basis when I was growing up and none of them had ever taken an interest in me nor said anything about loving me as Pretty Eyes Pastor had done. I wondered if he really cared about me. After all, if the mother of Jesus was married at twelve years old then it was possible that a grown man might love me and maybe he did choose me because God pointed me out so he could love me, as he had told me.

Thinking back in time, I had given him a glass of water in the pulpit a couple of years earlier while helping the junior nurses' board. When I walked past some of the church mothers sitting on the front pew, they gave me many smiles of approval and one of them told me the Bible says that anyone who gives a man of God a cup of water would surely be blessed and favored for serving him. It did seem that Pretty Eyes Preacher was favoring me.

I fell asleep many nights listening to my father's distant voice coming through the heating vent as he practiced his sermons downstairs in his basement office. My admiration for preachers reached all the way down the family line to the Deep South where I spent some of my summers when I was young, staying with my uncle who pastored two churches at the same time down there and his proper southern bell wife. On Saturday mornings, several preachers and deacons came over to the house for breakfast and I helped with preparing the food. Serving preachers and being in their presence was a common part of my life.

I was completely comfortable being around all of them because nothing had ever occurred that would have made me think any of them would ever harm me in any way. As a child, those strong men of God always seemed like an ark of safety for me. Pretty eyes Pastor changed my normal association with preachers into something that was unfamiliar and completely unexpected. My heart was concerned about him after I saw him cry and I just wanted to reach out with compassion. I did not understand how I ended up in a situation that would label me the biggest disgrace in the church if anyone ever found out about our involvement, according to Pretty Eyes Pastor.

Later, when I told Pretty Eyes Pastor my menstrual cycles had started, he completely lost all interest in any sexual activity with me, but remained cordial around my family. I was scheduled for my first female medical exam, but seeing the stirrups attached to the table and a male doctor terrified me. I never did complete a gynecological exam until after I was married.

Before he left town the last time I saw him until I

became an adult, my father said a prayer at church, then Pretty Eyes Pastor stepped up to the microphone and gave him a few compliments. Next, he asked me to stand up and told the church I had grown to be a wonderful respectful young lady who reflected the goodness of my father and he should be proud of me. Everyone in the congregation, including his wife who came unexpectedly, was looking at me; they were all clapping and shouting "Amen." I wanted to cry and run out but I was paralyzed with fear and just quietly sat back down. I could never destroy the proud happy smile on my father's face, especially knowing that everyone in church social circles always stereotyped the preacher's kids (PK) by saying they were the worst ones in the church.

Looking at my father's face reminded me of the day he stood in the baptismal pool with the pastor years earlier, I could hear an echo in my mind of his voice when he said, "I baptize you my sister in the name of the Father, the Son and the Holy Ghost." After they plunged me under the water, I came back up looking at the smile on my father's face as I wiped my eyes. My mother was there with a towel to wrap around me when I got out of the pool.

After Pretty Eyes Pastor asked me to stand up that day, I developed such a self-conscience fear of people looking at me when I walked into a room, that once in early adulthood I was required to attend an orientation class for a job, but when I saw others had arrived before me, I would not go inside. My subconscious had trained me to always arrive early everywhere and take a seat before anyone else. I lost the job.

Most people are impressed by emotional preaching far more often than true biblical teaching and within fifteen minutes of his sermons everyone was always on their feet responding to him. I felt ashamed, embarrassed and too afraid to say anything about our involvement. Nobody would have ever believed that a handsome married pastor had secret pedophile lust hidden within his heart, especially since there were so many adult women always trying to have sex with him. This was also during a time when the parishioners would have never believed so many handsome married men were secretly homosexuals. Everyone was always focused on his great whooping style of preaching and that was all they could relate to him.

I was truly a daddy's girl but during that time
I hated that my father was a preacher seeking to lead his own church. The disposition of people in church during that time would not have called for Pretty Eyes Pastor to be reprimanded for his conduct with a child; instead, everyone would have said it was shameful that a fast little girl was involved with a grown man. In addition, he took advantage of being able to use the judgmental opinions in the church to protect himself.

I liked Pretty Eyes Pastor long before any of this

began and had a sense of anticipation along with everyone else at the church when it was announced that he would be the guest speaker. Although I did not fully understand the scriptures, I knew everyone was excited when he would be teaching them.

Lacking adequate knowledge of adult issues, I was not able to decipher if my involvement with Pretty Eyes Preacher was really wrong or just confidential. Every home had issues they only discussed within their own family. It was not that the discussion was wrong; a child would be punished for talking about what was discussed because they breached a family confidence.

I had so many questions that I wanted answered, but I did not have anyone I could confide in about the situation, if I started asking too many adult questions then someone might become suspicious. I lived in constant fear because I could not tell anyone or that someone would discover what happened on their own and I lived in constant fear of being spiritually damned if I did reveal our sacred secret.

I withdrew from my friends and became a shy quiet introvert developing a terrible nail biting habit that often left my nail beds bleeding. Since I could not talk to anyone about my feelings, I wrote about them in my diary every day. The adults were saying that various unexplainable phases in mood and behavior were normal during the adolescent years. When I decided to remain quiet, I assumed the weight of a burden that nearly crushed my young spirit to death.

During my high school years, I went to visit with one of the sick church mother's right before she died. She had the greatest gospel voice I had ever heard in my life. For no apparent reason, she told me her generation was accustom to seeing a child in most homes that could not do anything except sit on the couch rocking back and forth all day long because they were born as a result of incest. She said having sex with grown men was "the cross young girls had to bear" when he was the provider. The men of God were the spiritual and social providers in the community, visiting the sick, raising money for funerals, feeding the hungry and helping to provide anything else a family might need.

A producer recorded an album of her singing. When she was young, her parents knew that somewhere along the road that she would be required to have sex with adult men in the business including pastors who would invite her to sing at their churches, and she did. Never looking at me the entire time she spoke, in a sorrowful low tone of voice, she mentioned seeing me in the church basement once back when Pretty Eyes Pastor was playing around with me feeling on my legs. It seemed the devastation older women had experienced with men made them bitter toward the younger women and they secretly wanted to see us suffer as they did. Who were we to escape pain? I did not know what to think, but for a moment, I stopped feeling like a secretive sinful shameful fool after hearing that some other young girls had been in the same situation and I felt a sense of being a normal person.

My actions were not an active attempt to progress in life "fast" beyond my age. During those years, social value was determined by who wanted to be one of your associates. Pretty Eyes Preacher was someone who was popular and loved by everyone. As a young lady, I was not sure what his interest in me said about my personal value. I had a normal curiosity about the type of person that I was developing into and did not know how to access the situation correctly.

The extremely high number of single mothers should be enough evidence to prove that adult women repeatedly make the wrong decisions about men. Therefore, I fail to understand how adults justify blaming minors for making wrong decisions when they have been sexually abused knowing that their minds are not even fully developed and mature.

CHAPTER THREE

EMOTIONAL DESTRUCTION

Sometimes, after a significant amount of time has passed, an abuser will apologize to the victim, but at other times the abuser will never admit to guilt and attempt to make the victim feel responsible

I was fourteen years old the last time I had seen Pretty Eyes Pastor. Aside from finding ways to avoid attending revival until I became an adult, I was socializing with my friends once again and pursuing my interest in younger men who were closer to my age.

When we saw each other again at revival, my father had since died. There was a time I wanted to tell my father about Pretty Eyes Pastor but his health was unstable. Concerned about his future, I did not want his last thoughts to be that he had not been a good father. Right after graduating from high school I had been in a bad marriage that failed primarily because I kept the sexual abuse hidden from my ex-husband and could not resolve my issues secretly while in a marriage. I was never able to either overcome the shame of my childhood or gain the courage to risk finding out what his reaction might be. Often, when spouses do not reveal serious issues before getting married, it could turn out badly later. I was still very nonsocial with strangers in high school but he was able to connect with me in spite of my quietness. I was afraid of losing a man who found value in my life and that fear ended up causing me to lose the relationship. I had become another statistic among the high number of women whose marriage had ended in divorce after they were sexually abused as a child.

I did not have any interest in Pretty Eyes Pastor, by this time I realized that his pretty eyes were not as magical as they appeared when I was young. The only reason I went to church that night was to support my friends who were singing in a gospel group.

As usual, the church was filled to capacity with people who loved to hear him preach. During the service, a few police officers from the area were standing in the back during their lunch break. Within fifteen minutes of his sermon, everyone was standing in response to his dramatic arrangement of eloquent words and gestures. The ushers were fanning people who were dancing around, but in my mind, he did not appear to be the great supernatural orator that I once thought he was and whom everyone referred to as being back when I was young. It all seemed to be nothing more than a deceitful show to me. I could not identify with nor realize any divine awareness and connection to God from his preaching.

When the service was over, I did not even stay around in the sanctuary to speak. After socializing in the dining area everyone left the church and I bumped into Pretty Eyes Pastor in the parking lot. He asked if I would take a short ride with him so we could talk. I should have followed my first instinct and said, NO.

I was a young woman in my early twenties wearing a skirt above my knees with a short sleeve cashmere sweater and sandals. Because the weather was so nice, putting on pantyhose was out of the question for me.

He parked on a residential street that was somewhat secluded and only had one streetlight, then lit a cigarette. After sitting there for about fifteen minutes without either one of us saying a single word, I thought he might have wanted to apologize for the sexual encounters when I was young and maybe it was difficult to find the words. I asked him if that was the reason he wanted to talk with me. The expression on his face turned into pure rage.

He reached over me and pulled the seat release, held me down with one arm across my chest while he pulled my panties down. Then he climbed on top of me and used his weight to hold me down while he unzipped his pants as I struggled to push him away and repeatedly shouted at him to stop.

A few minutes later, I heard a familiar sigh of

relief coming from him that directed my thoughts away from the immediate situation for a moment and caused my memory to travel backward in time to remember the night I had been in the car with him when I was twelve years old. He looked at me and said that whatever happened back then did not matter anymore because I was an adult having sex with him now.

He rolled back over into the driver's seat and continued to smoke his cigarette. I just sat in the passenger seat staring without saying a word. Right at that moment a police car rode past. I reached for the door to jump out, but he yanked my arm and told me not to be a fool because those officers had been at the church to hear him preach and they would not believe anything that I had to say. I knew that his statement was probably correct. They were familiar with the people from the church and there had been times when they came for a domestic situation in the neighborhood and all they did was convince the complainant not to have their family or friends arrested.

CHICAGO-December 8, 2009
Victims of sexual abuse by priests share shocking stories *"We put them (priest) on pedestals almost to the point where I thought they were more than superhuman in a sense.... When he went to the Chicago Police, they called him a liar and laughed at him"*[1]

It has been said that community policing will

help the citizens feel more secure and allow the police to become familiar with the community. Sometimes the police form an opinion about certain people and they act out of bias not necessarily on facts.

He forcefully grabbed his briefcase off the backseat and took a Bible out that had two old love letters folded within the pages that I had written to him when I was young. He said if I told anyone that he had forced himself on me the letters would prove to everyone that I had been in love with him since I was a child and that I had longed to be with him sexually for years. Everyone at the church would hate me for making those allegations because they all held him in high regard and some had even taken time off from work to come hear him preach.

The feelings of personal degradation overtook my heart as he spoke in an arrogant condescending tone of voice reminding me of his high level of respect and honor within the church and that my accusations would not have any merit with anyone. They would only cause me to appear to be a vengeful woman who was trying to destroy his credibility. I sat with my head bowed down the entire time he was speaking.

I could not believe that he engaged me in emotional and sexual situations with his charming manipulating personality when I was young that were morally and legally wrong, and then kept my letters to use as a weapon against me in defense of his wrongdoing.

He told me to clean myself up as he drove off taking me back to my car. I was getting out of the car when he grabbed my arm and angrily said he was disappointed that I grew up to be a harlot that would screw a man outside in a car. There was so much turmoil inside of my heart that I could not even speak to give a response.

"But he refused to listen to her, and since he was stronger than she, he raped her. Then Amnon hated her with intense hatred. In fact, he hated her more than he had loved her. Amnon said to her, "Get up and get out!" 2 Samuel 13:14-15 (NIV)

The next five days I did not go to work or even call in sick. I was just lying in the bed under the covers and I do not even remember using the bathroom for the entire time. A friend from my job asked the building manager to open my door. I just laid there trembling and did not respond to any questions.

After not being able to communicate effectively with anyone, I was taken to a psychiatric hospital for a while. The doctor assigned me to a suicide watch room where someone monitored my activity all day and night. There were group therapy sessions with ten people and a brief visit from the doctor every day, but that was not enough activity to keep my mind occupied. I did not smoke cigarettes and even with adjusted doses, the SSRI antidepressants did not provide any relief from my anxiety; the medication only gave me constant headaches. I was still depressed, anxious and confused when my hospital stay ended. However, the doctor was required to discharge me after I reached the maximum amount of days that my insurance would cover for medical costs.

When my pastor visited me in the hospital, we discussed everything that occurred since I had been twelve years old. After praying for me, he said that it was all over now and that I should just let the Lord deal with Pretty Eyes Pastor.

I tried to simply forgive and move on with my life. However, there was a special program at church the following month and the scheduled guest preacher cancelled. Then I heard that Pretty Eyes Pastor would be coming in his place.

Upset and fearful, I asked my pastor why he did not inform me of this when he knew that I had only been out of the hospital for a few weeks and I was still struggling emotionally. He responded in a very dogmatic tone of voice saying, "I am the pastor and I am not required to inform anyone about the decisions I make at my church. There is nothing that can be done about the past because it would be your word against Pretty Eyes Pastor and more people would support him, so just shut up and thank God that it is all over. Because even if he were sitting in the electric chair about to be executed he would be declaring his innocence as the switch was being turned on"

After inquiring about the new list of prayer partners at the church, he became even angrier while warning me not to repeat what happened with Pretty Eyes Pastor to anyone else. I was taken to the emergency room after having a panic attack that caused extremely severe chest pain the week Pretty Eyes Pastor was scheduled to preach at the church.

It was impossible to endure another day with misdirected thoughts scattered around in my mind and it seemed that prayer, the church, nor any doctor was able to help me. I felt betrayed by the church and believed the man of God had taken advantage of me sexually then completely mislead me when my mind was not mature enough to make proper judgments. Everyone lovingly praised him while not giving a damn about what was happening to me. It appeared that every wrong thing he did was minimized or disregarded and any turmoil that I was experiencing was my own fault for not forgetting about the past.

I made up my mind to forget the past forever. That night, I sat holding my handgun for over an hour while I searched my mind for a solution to resolve my pain. I did not simply want to run away from the issues in my mind. I wanted to find a resolution that would give me some peace, but I could not find any answers.

I had reached the final point of confusion and could not tolerate any more harassing thoughts torturing me over my involvement with Pretty Eyes Pastor.

I had given in to his request when I was a child because I loved him and I thought he loved me because God wanted to express love to me through him and now I believed God was expressing hatred, anger and disgust toward me through him.

I pointed the gun at myself and then stopped to think if this was the only way to escape my pain. I could not find another solution. I chambered a round. I pointed the gun at myself again and pulled the trigger. The strong force from the impact of the bullet thrust my body off the chair like a ragdoll propelling downward violently crashing against the floor. When I finally opened my eyes to see medical staff attempting to save my life, I did not feel any gratitude. The only feelings I had were anger and disgust because I did not resolve my emotional pain and grief. If I had been able to verbalize my feelings, I would have cursed the staff and God for keeping me alive.

Members of the clergy are permitted to visit hospital patients at any time; my frustration only became worse when my pastor walked into the room. I laid there with my eyes fixed on his cynical facial expression as he leaned over the bed nearly touching my face speaking in a displeasing tone of voice, telling me that I was just going from mess to mess and that I was too young to ruin my life completely. If anyone knew that I had become mentally unstable enough to attempt suicide over uncontrolled emotions related to Pretty Eyes Pastor, they would support and protect him after escaping involvement with a crazy woman. Unmarried men in the church would never risk becoming involved in a relationship with me and I could never seek a viable career because my background records would permanently reflect that I was a psychiatric patient.

My eyes continued to be firmly focused on him as his tone of voice and facial expression changed into controlling authority. He sternly repeated the same question three times: *"I believe that you just had an accident while handling the gun, didn't you?"*

I shook my head to indicate that I was saying "NO" the first two times. Then the third time he angrily asked, I began crying and I shook my head saying *"YES."*

Attempting to limit interacting with anyone and to avoid realizing the effects of my emotional pain now combined with physical pain, for the rest of my hospital stay I self-dispensed sedating pain medication constantly until the doctor moved the pump out of my reach. That was the first time in my entire life I had been in the hospital with an injury. I went home about thirty days later after having multiple surgeries and blood transfusions.

I was not a member of the same church where my family attended, which was where Pretty Eyes Pastor's inappropriate behavior started in the church basement when I was a child.

However, pastors under the same denominational organization all associated together and when my pastor met with their pastors to discuss my situation, they decided Pretty Eyes Pastor's church members would be upset and too many other people would be hurt if anyone became aware of the sexual abuse. Therefore, the best resolution was to keep praying asking the Lord to work out the situation and leave the past behind.

A survivor of clergy child sexual abuse has endured a type of injustice that cannot be resolved solely within the confines of spirituality any more than someone attacked on the street should be told not to call the police because the Lord will handle the situation.

This was during an era when many pastors' wives did not have any individuality and their sole identity was connected to their position of being the first lady of the church. Many were willing to remain quiet about wrong behavior in order to help their husbands remain in their position to ensure they maintained their first lady title and lifestyle. Since Pretty Eyes Pastor's church had taken out a million dollar loan for a building project, they needed to maintain his leadership to ensure the membership level and annual finances remained intact.

There is a standard saying among pastors when controversy is forming. If you give attention to the situation then it will become important but if you treat the situation as if it is nothing then it will become nothing. It has become normal to hear clergy attempting to make sexual abuse committed by other clergy seem unimportant by claiming they are just human beings and they fall short like any other man. Although the time allowed for statutory rape had passed, there was a different law governing those in a position of authority and trust. I was over eighteen years old, but still within the age boundaries for reporting under the other law. The pastors chose to conceal, ignore and manipulate everyone involved with scriptures in order to overlook to situation and protect their clergy friend.

None of the pastors ever said another word to me about what happened. The deacons and the board members from the churches never said another word about what happened. My pastor asked me to work around the church every day. Each time I had an emotional breakdown over Pretty Eyes Pastor, he reminded me in an angry tone of voice about the scandals on television with men in positions of power and how the women always lost their respect along with many career opportunities while the men continued with their normal life.
I found out later that my pastor and my family's pastor were communicating on a regular basis

and informing Pretty Eyes Pastor of everything I said about him. While I remained unemployed for over two years, neither of the pastors was even kind enough to offer me a free chicken dinner to eat. They continued with their lives disregarding everything that occurred and ignored or minimized any effects the situation had on my life.

Pretty Eyes Pastor continued speaking as a guest revivalist at the churches and my pastor completed an expansion on his church. Having me work at the church without pay to keep me occupied while emotionally chastising me was nothing but a maneuver by the pastors to remain aware of my legal intensions and to deter me from seeking recourse. Whenever I mentioned anything related to Pretty Eyes Pastor, my pastor became like a parent using anger to intimidate a child from talking about a specific situation.

A couple of years later I learned that Pretty Eyes Pastor fathered a child with a young lady who was barely an adult and it had been rumored that he was involved with her when she was a minor. Nevertheless, if he were in jail then he would not have been able to give large child support payments nor make sure the church kept making loan repayments. The need for him to produce great financial outcomes far exceeded the need for him to produce great moral outcomes.

Those holy board members who supported preachers who encouraged people to sacrifice and give money to the church that they really needed, then trust God to find another way to pay their bills, were not themselves willing to sacrifice and remove a pedophile from his position, then trust God to find another way to pay the church mortgage.

CHAPTER FOUR

DAMAGE FROM CHURCH POLITICS

Sometimes, when feelings that have been buried alive rise up again, they can be used to construct a new life instead of being allowed to be a destructive force

I woke up early one morning feeling pain and discomfort in an area near the gunshot wound that had not bothered me in many years. When the bullet entered, it shattered into many pieces and the fragments remain inside of my body.

More than twenty years had passed since my suicide attempt and when I was younger my body appeared to heal very well, but I was aging and the overall condition of my health was changing.

I went to the doctor seeking some form of pain relief and he told me there were new types of modern laser technology that could provide many options that were not available in the past. I desperately wanted to learn about all the different procedures but I faced a major obstacle. Since this was a pre-existing condition, my insurance would not cover the cost for elective procedures.

I felt like I was being abused, raped and degraded all over again. After so many years had passed away, I was confronted with repercussions from the past while everyone else who was involved had forgotten all about me and the pain that I suffered. Recently, I had gone back to the church where Pretty Eyes Pastor began playing around with his hands under my dress grooming me for the abuse when I was young, to attend a funeral for a senior family member.

When I walked past to view the body, the retired pastor was shaking hands with everyone. He looked at me and said, "I have not seen you in so long that I forgot you were a relative. What is your name again"? I attempted to kill myself over abuse that started at his church with a preacher he always invited as a guest speaker and sent him to stay at our home. He concealed the matter all those years ago and now he had forgotten my name.

Over the years, I continued attending church, praying, praising God and trying to keep hope alive believing that everything was going to be all right, but it never did become all right. Every year was composed of daily struggles to find hope in life with an occasional short-term run of encouragement, but I did not know which days I would have the strength to carry out my daily routine or which days I would feel weak and just lay in bed. I led such a secluded lifestyle that it was extremely rare for me to have any issues with anyone other than myself.

I tried to deal with the entire abuse situation from a secular point of view as if someone had betrayed me at an old job that I would never need again and supervisors from the past that would never be important in my life again. However, having a church home and a pastor would always be an important part of my life. I could not simply forget the events that surrounded my spiritual life.

The men who were given the responsibility of directing my soul and being great teachers in my life had been the very men who contributed to my near self-destruction and that was still having an effect on me. I did not realize the severe effects the abuse had on my relationship with God. My view of love and trust had been distorted, but the depth of the effects were intensified because my perception changed after the men whom I believed exemplified the attributes of God treated me in a wrongful manner.

I harbored secret offense and resentment in my heart toward God and his church. Hearing preachers and great gospel voices sing songs that said God was in control of my life caused me to wonder why he did not prevent the childhood abuse, which would have prevented this entire destructive cycle from even starting.

It was hurtful knowing that Pretty Eyes Pastor had used his friendship with my father to gain my trust in order to take advantage of me sexually and then realizing that every word he spoke, every gesture he made and every action he took was a manipulating lie.

They were merely an assortment of selfish manipulating actions strategically executed to fulfill his own secret lust and to protect him from disgrace after fulfilling his forbidden desires, and to block me from learning the truth about things in life that he said I already knew.

The pastors may have concealed the matter because of some minor concern for my wellbeing; but the true motive behind the concealment was to help them avoid judgment according to the same moral standards they imposed on others. They quickly disregarded their integrity and lowered their standards in private to benefit themselves in public and protect their good paying pastor jobs at my emotional, physical, spiritual and sexual expense.

They allowed human weakness to be used as an acceptable reason to overlook Pretty Eyes Pastor's failure to uphold his legal and moral responsibility. He was in a position of authority and caused harm to my life. In reality, he had been a criminal in hiding that was able to escape conviction with the assistance of his accomplices, fellow pastors, who were men representing God. Spirituality must be handled with responsibility;

it does not eliminate the right to seek earthly justice, which has time limitations as opposed to spiritual justice. Lest every preacher would petition the courts not to prosecute any criminal who was a baptized believer and just allow the Lord to impose a sentence.

There were a number of self-destructive feelings that I handled incorrectly, which caused me to have a dysfunctional relationship with God. Since God is omnipresent, I could not simply avoid a phone call or a doorbell but I did withdraw from God except for the times when it was necessary to communicate. Acting like an angry child who could not leave their parents' home so they just stay in their room with the door closed. In hindsight, I was able to see this behavior limited my progress in life and I willfully restrained myself until I made the decision to repair my relationship with God and come out of my room.

I suffered anxiety each time I remembered the trauma in my life that God failed to control as the preachers at church said he would. He allowed it to occur in my life when it was within his power, but he did not care enough about me to keep me from harm.

The severe headaches from the stress and anguish of knowing that he failed to protect me were almost debilitating because they could not be relieved with medication. If the greatest power I knew would turn his back on me, then there was nothing else for me to hope for in life. The anger, frustration and sadness lingered on for years.

I only opened my eyes every morning because I did not have any other choice. Usually I did not socialize with anyone on my job. I performed my assigned task daily and even received company recognition for going beyond the call of duty. Later, when I arrived home, I would fall down and lie on the kitchen floor sobbing all night at times.

I had conditioned myself to endure the attacks from the internal mental war in my mind. The comparison of my self-worth against the value of my abuser's never ceased. Thoughts of me being an insignificant human being who could be killed and nobody would care while my abuser was being held in high esteem being praised and honored caused me so much emotional pain that at times my crying spells were uncontrollable.

My anger grew toward God for keeping me alive every time I heard a rousing applause with people shouting Amen at the mention of my abuser's name. I felt offended and angry like a mother whose child was murdered, then the offender escapes conviction because of political connections and then they become the head of the police department, a violator of safety in charge of safety for the entire city.

All pastors are in a position that will allow them to perform many good deeds that are greater than their true level of concern for others and it was difficult for me to accept knowing they could use those deeds as a tool to shield themselves from the consequences of wrong behavior. Many public displays, especially in front of the media, are important strategies to help them secure their good paying jobs.

The view of leadership has changed in the church and I often hear some pastors refer to themselves as the CEO. I have a problem with the church adapting this view because when products are damaged a business can write it off as a loss, and I felt written off as a loss after I was damaged and the operation of the business continued as normal.

The church is required to meet financial obligations just as any other organization. However, some pastors have used their position as an opportunity to propel their career and make them the head of a Fortune 500 church, with little or no real dedication to the Bible or people, just buying prewritten sermons from religious speech and sermon writing services to read with charm and eloquence from the pulpit.

Company	Church
CEO/President	Pastor
*********************	******************
Customers	*Church Members*
Visibility in the target market: Billboards, signs on the sides of buses, etc.	***Visibility in the target market:*** Attend protests, marches, high profile funerals covered by media, etc.
Profit reports: If low, develop new marketing strategies to sell more products	*Finance reports:* If low, develop new sermon strategies to bring in larger offerings
Seasonal specific promotions to increase sales: Holiday season, Valentine's Day, etc.	*Seasonal specific sermons to receive larger offerings:* Emotional sermons to older congregants during holidays, Mother's Day, etc. Will usually result in large emotional giving
Damaged items: Write off losses in annual taxes	***EMOTIONALY/SPIRITUALY DAMAGED PEOPLE:*** Effective outreach team to increase membership and replace losses

Most pastors are wonderful leaders who are more than worthy of the benefits they receive and many are even undercompensated when they remain focused on the true mission of the church. The wonderful pastors who have been a part of my life over the years played a crucial role in my decision not to completely lose faith in the church. They continued to show me how to utilize the church for what it provides and not leave over what it is lacking.

They help me to understand the church is not some form of earthly heaven where you can escape from the problems and troubles in life. The members are not angels full of holiness and good intensions toward everyone; the pastor is not Jesus who is able to walk on water with godliness. Dispel the myth that everything you need to live and resolve your problems can all be found within your church and if you pray then prayer will fix everything for you. The same people who work at secular jobs cheating on time cards, stealing items, gossiping, gathering in cliques and whatever else are the same people who make up the environment at church and they bring their same attitudes into the building with them.

We can only hope that most of the people come together to support each other while gaining a better understanding of how to live by the word of God. Anyone who engages in sex with a child would have the same secret lustful desires even if they worked as a bus driver instead of a pastor; their position cannot be connected to their desires.

There are times when we need assistance outside of the church or maybe just outside of our home church. Preaching and praying is very different from effective counseling and life restructuring. If another church has something I need then utilize it when I need it, pastors should not be afraid to give members a letter transferring them to another church for a while and should be able to recommend where they should go or call another pastor to let them know they are sending one of the members to be under their spiritual care. I appreciate all of the support pastors have given me and I did not lose faith in clergy as a whole even after everything that occurred because of their positive influence in my life during a critical time.

After I was unable to utilize any of the new procedures that were available to relieve my physical pain, I consulted with an attorney who told me that if I had initiated legal action within the time allowed then my abuser could have been held responsible for my medical bills, but the statute of limitations had expired. When I began searching for legal answers there was some debate over the liability of the church that was paying my abuser to be in town as their guest speaker. Were they only liable for his inappropriate behavior at the church or elsewhere as well? Illinois law could not be enforced against the church where my abuser was the pastor because it was located out of state. The question was asked that if a traveling salesman assaults a child while working out of state then what liability would the employer hold.

The next statement the attorney made turned out to be the action I needed to take in order to point me in the right direction for my life.
He informed me that there were new child sexual assault bills pending in the legislature and the testimony of a survivor could be a powerful personal statement that could have an impact on the passage of new laws.

In the event that I had not resolved all the feelings I had buried alive years ago, this would give me the opportunity to evaluate their strength in my life. I was determined not to allow them to turn into a destructive force that was controlling me. Instead, I was going to channel them into a direction where the response from the demonstration of their power might result in a positive life-changing experience.

I was not working and lost my insurance coverage after the suicide attempt. I never sought professional counseling again. I did not talk about what happened with anyone else for nearly twenty years because I knew that everyone had their own problems. From the beginning stages of my personal trauma, it seemed that nobody cared and those who were concerned just did not know what to say or what to do. Therefore, talking about the trauma seemed to be pointless.

I had already learned an important life lesson about the clergy code of silence, discovering that I could not even rely on assistance from my own pastor when the problem was with a fellow clergyman within their networking clique of churches where they obtained preaching engagements for additional income. I was foolish to believe that because those men were members of the clergy, moral persuasion would have an equal amount of power as the law in their lives causing them to act on their knowledge of illegal activity. History continues to be repeated by showing the church fails at self-discipline.

Now I had the opportunity to share my painful experience in a forum where my voice would matter to someone. I definitely knew the time for me to speak had arrived. The pending bill was the exact bill that would have allowed me to receive some form of justice for the emotional and physical trauma that I endured at the hands of my abuser. Even though many years had already gone past and it was not a part of law during the years that I was abused, my voice had a chance to affect the lives of other victims by helping to ensure their abuser would not escape accountability for their actions if a victim required a lengthy amount of time to heal and gain emotional strength before they could expose their abuser or if the church concealed their abuse.

I fully understood why victims are fearful of talking about the details of their personal sexual trauma in front of a room full of people including media reporters who do not have anything to do with legislative decisions. When the legislature requested my testimony, I could barely speak through the tears and I had to pause continually in the beginning. Nevertheless, I knew that I had to withstand the actions of my emotions and keep speaking to accomplish my purpose for being there. The compassionate ladies from the sexual assault organization were right by my side providing moral support. The devastating power from the emotions that resulted after my abuse reached out and penetrated the minds of the decision makers.

The bill passed with a unanimous vote!

I had a wonderful feeling of justice for one (me) and justice for all (victims) on behalf of those who faced the same opposition that I had and who took their own lives to escape the pain, as I had attempted. With all the changes made within the legal system as new leaders assume various positions, I hope those victims rest in peace. As attitudes change with each generation, there are new attempts to prevent other victims from believing the only escape from their pain is through death or destructive behavior because they are worthless and powerless against their abuser.

The survivors have access to legal power when they find the inner strength to exercise their rights. All deserve to be granted ample time to heal in each individual situation.

However, in a bittersweet twist of fate, just a few

months later there was media coverage about the police station in the same suburban town where I did not report my sexual assault after seeing officers standing in the back of the church to hear my abuser preach. The local county police discovered several rape kits sitting in a room that had never been tested dating back nearly twenty years. Although there was a DNA match on one test to a criminal in the national database, they faced limitations because the statute of limitations had expired. The article stated if the current new law had been in effect, the law I gave my testimony for, the state would have been able to prosecute and seek justice for the victims in all of the cases. I did not know any of the other victims and nobody knew their cases had been treated as though they were insignificant and that the police had disregarded the crimes against them. My heart was reassured that I had made the correct decision to end my silence and speak out with my testimony to compel passing the new law. Even if I had reported the crime all those years ago, my rape kit would probably have been just sitting in the room with all of the others.

The old process of allowing behavior that harms someone's life to be judged according to the level of integrity within each individual church is just as ridiculous as running a company based on moral character without outside regulation and laws to control its operation effectively.

A Christian belief is the church should be perfect

without spot nor wrinkle when Jesus returns to earth. Until that time comes, when pastors and the church have violated the law, people cannot be afraid to utilize the justice system against them to expose and correct its spots and wrinkles.

I believe the government should form a department for religious organizations nationwide that is similar to the Better Business Bureau, where records of allegations are recorded and the church must respond with the action taken to address the problem. An external recordkeeping system would assist attorneys, prosecutors and social services.

Each denomination can set rules for itself. For example, if an associate minister at a church applies for a federal chaplain position, the president of the denomination must authorize a letter of endorsement on behalf of the minister.
The president of each denominational organization is not liable for anything that occurs within each individual church. The organization provides medical, retirement benefits, etcetera for pastors and a general set of "self-made" rules, beliefs, doctrines, practices and bylaws, etcetera but does not monitor activity at individual churches.

The Ecclesiastical Baptist Faith organizations recognized by the U.S. Government (2013) are listed below. All other non-recognized groups are considered "religious cults"

1. Alliance of Baptists, Inc.
2. American Baptist Association
3. American Baptist Churches USA
4. Baptist Bible Fellowship International
5. Baptist General Conference (Converge Worldwide)
6. Baptist General Convention of Texas
7. Baptist General Convention of Virginia
8. Baptist Missionary Association of America
9. Conservative Baptist Association of America
10. Cooperative Baptist Fellowship Inc.
11. Full Gospel Baptist Church Fellowship International
12. General Association of General Baptist Churches
13. General Association of Regular Baptist Churches
14. Liberty Baptist Fellowship for Church Planting, Inc.
15. National Association of Free Will Baptists
16. National Baptist Convention of America, Inc.
17. National Missionary Baptist Convention of America
18. National Baptist Convention USA, Inc.
19. New Testament Association of Independent Baptist Churches
20. North American Baptist Conference
21. Original Free Will Baptists Convention
22. Progressive National Baptist Convention, Inc.
23. Seventh-Day Baptists General Conference
24. Southern Baptist Convention
25. Sovereign Grace Baptist Association
26. Unaffiliated Baptist Churches of America
27. World Baptist Fellowship, Inc.

This is only the list for the Baptist faith. There will never be control over abuse while every individual church under each different organization and under each different faith can self-regulate and self-report without any universal guidelines to be enforced.

Clergy in many states are designated "mandatory reporters" of child abuse that is not revealed to them while the abuser is seeking spiritual advice. Although, they are not required to have background checks themselves. This is a complete contradiction since we know that many of them are the offenders. Even with all the nationwide media exposure, some members of the clergy continue to abuse children sexually.

Pedophile clergy are aware of the methods used to manipulate the system and utilize the religious privilege loopholes in the law to conceal their illegal acts. They know many people trust the holiness symbolized by the collar around their neck. I spent many years working around convicts and all career criminals had a common characteristic. They diligently studied in the law library, researched books or newspapers and received advice from other criminals to help them construct a plan to evade the police during crimes they planned to commit in the future.

Each time a church group came to visit, they discussed details of each person all the way down to the shoes they wore, to determine which type of people they should insist are removed from the jury selection by their attorney, so they would have a greater chance of escaping conviction giving them freedom to commit more crimes.

Everywhere else in society there are state or federal laws to monitor employees who have direct contact with children and impose fines on employers who violate the law. Each of these denominational organizations have the freedom to decide their own rules and regulations. Most do not even conduct background checks on clergy and church employees. They decide their own requirements without any oversight from outside the church. They are autonomous within their affiliated denominational organization and the community, only being required to meet standard city codes for public safety. Many have paid the price with their spiritual life and literal human life for the costs incurred when the church abuses its religious privileges.

Each territory must contain and control the epidemic of clergy sexual abuse, as it crosses all denominational lines and occurs around the world.

BRAZIL—January 28, 2013 Evangelical pastor convinced followers his penis contained holy milk. *Valdeci Sobrino Picanto is a Brazilian evangelical pastor. He has been arrested after deceiving the faithful using the name of the "Holy Spirit." By using these foolish lies this criminal pastor claimed that the Holy Spirit would secrete from his penis in the form of "sacred milk." This pastor said that his penis was blessed and that "the Lord had consecrated him with divine milk of the Holy Spirit" and, of course, he had to release it in order to "evangelize." "He has convinced us that only God could come into our lives through our mouth and that's why he would do what he did." Often, after worship, pastor Valdeci would take us to where the funds were kept at the back of the church and asked us to have oral sex with him until the Holy Spirit would come through ejaculation." This is the testimony of one of his victims.* [2]

These types of disgraceful sexually abusive situations occurring inside the house of the Lord further prove my belief that members in some churches, usually women, have such a desperate need to support and believe in an alleged good man that they will forsake intelligent thinking. They allow biased distorted views to control their emotions and religious connections, just as they do when involved in destructive personal relationships. I seriously doubt there were many adult Christian men who condoned and were willing to receive the Holy Spirit through sacred ejaculation. The power clergy have over children has been given to them by adults.

The occurrence of child sexual abuse in a public place of worship is a violation of public safety. The church is never justified for settling matters internally that fall under the guidelines of criminal law when an offense has been committed against a minor. Children are at greater risk of experiencing adverse effects in the future when they do not feel validated and safe.

The range of different criminal charges for sexual abusers can vary in different states:
- aggravated indecent assault,
- child sexual abuse,
- indecency with a child/sexual contact,
- involuntary deviate sexual intercourse with a child,
- rape 2,
- reckless corruption of a minor,
- reckless endangerment of a minor,
- sodomy,
- statutory sexual assault,
- unlawful contact with a minor,
- unlawful restraint of a minor and
- unlawful transaction with a minor and use of an electronic communications system to procure a minor for a sexual offense.

Some of the most common adverse effects a victim displays because of sexual abuse are:
- anxiety,
- anorexia,
- attention deficit hyperactivity disorder,
- bulimia nervosa,
- complex post-traumatic stress disorder,
- depression,
- further victimization in adulthood,
- low Scholastic Aptitude Test (SAT),
- obesity (often leads to diabetes) and
- social isolation.

The State of Illinois has passed Senate Bill 1399

eliminating the civil statute of limitations for sex offenses committed against minors and House Bill 1063, which eliminates the criminal statute of limitations. Thirty-three other states have eliminated their statute of limitations or extended the time for reporting sex offenses against minors.

The laws have changed across the country after clergy sexual abuse survivors and supporting organizations demanded revisions to the law. This is only one area where child sexual abuse occurs. There are a number of resources that need to be established and utilized to prevent and address various issues related to child sexual abuse. They will never become available until those who are willing to participate in a corporate calling to serve together in this designated area initiate some form of action.

Adults are responsible for the safety and security of minors. We can all contribute to our responsibility on some level whether we actively participate or support an organization in carrying out their mission. Some action must be taken to cultivate the future of our society and community.

Lastly, I would like to make one point clear. The child victims and adult survivors, who reveal, discuss and initiate changes in awareness and responses to child sexual abuse are not causing the church or clergy to have a negative image in the community. The clergy who are committing and attempting to hide these acts are the ones responsible for causing a negative reflection on the institution of the church and the office of the clergy as a whole.

CHAPTER FIVE

THE ROAD TO RECOVERY WITH EFT

Sometimes, the gift of freedom can bring challenges that are not present when you are securely locked away, but these things must be faced in order to live in total liberation

I was a young woman when I lost my way along the emotional road of life. After spending many years of being self-confined within myself, I did not walk out into freedom as a fully functioning healthy Christian during the initial stage of my liberation. The common testimony that everyone in church has heard before by people who declare, "Whatever God does in my life it's all right with me and I wouldn't change a thing" did not reflect my feelings. If I had a chance to go back in time I would have changed everything.

My release from self-confinement could be compared to a newly released convict that has to make adjustments when they return to living in society. A person who has been locked inside of their self has lived by similar mental restrictions just as someone who is physically locked inside of a jail.

Imagining that God would automatically create a perfectly peaceful life for me, I learned the same lesson that some of my coworkers were taught by God during the era of the "prosperity gospel" when they were waiting for someone to ring their doorbell and a miracle bag of money from God would be sitting on their doorstep.

While everyone has seen stories on the news about someone who has found a bag of money thrown into their backyard by a criminal trying to evade the police, those are exceptional situations. The path to financial freedom is a process requiring steps that must be followed.

Likewise, the path to lasting emotional freedom required that I follow a process of steps. This does not mean that people cannot receive miracle healings for their emotions. Not everyone will experience a miracle and this is the process I followed to reach the point that others may have received miraculously. It was a challenge to fully trust God, the church and myself again. Whenever I faced a situation that seemed like God or the church did not care or when someone seemed to demand a conversation from me after being quiet and withdrawn for so long, I wanted to retreat into the security of isolated self-confinement.

I used the modified version of the twelve steps to recovery that are used by recovering substance abusers along with emotional freedom techniques (EFT). This is based on the same energy meridians used in traditional acupuncture to treat physical and emotional ailments, but without the use of needles. Instead, tapping with the fingertips to input kinetic energy onto specific body meridians is the technique used. During the first month, I was still experiencing the effects of deeply hidden emotional pain during the EFT that I struggled to say the words, but the continued decrease in the pain while speaking helps to evaluate progress.

I acknowledged that I became distant from God because one of his ordained earthly representatives sexually abused me. I believed that I would have drawn closer to him if my abuser had not been a member of the clergy, and that distance only caused me to mistreat myself and speak abusive language into my spirit. Now, I am able to recognize and immediately address self-abusive behavior before it becomes destructive.

Step 1: I admitted that I became powerless to destructive emotions and I allowed them to take control until my life became unbearable. I did not believe that I had any issues over the years. I simply defined my self-confinement as an adult case of shyness.

Action: I decided to verbally communicate with God on a daily basis and speak positive words into my spirit, which was a challenge. Each time I said "I am a good person" I could feel my spirit rejecting my words because it took time for me to actually believe that those words were true.

Attempting to state positive affirmations and prayers of gratitude were not successful because they conflicted with the real deep true feelings I had about myself. Successful EFT required that I address why I did not believe a particular statement, then work through that specific issue. I initiated the EFT phrases until I felt a shift in feelings (energy). Then I followed daily and weekly plans. If completely honest phrases are said during EFT there will be an immediate feeling of shifting. All of the specific issues related to one particular area causing the blockage take a significant amount of time to reveal and work through.

Ever since childhood, I heard preachers continually say that Christians cannot evaluate spiritual progress by their feelings. Then, the same preacher would say that they would not have a religion they could not feel sometimes. I never understood these contradictory statements. EFT is one of the correct ways that feelings can be utilized to evaluate progress. Maybe you do not believe that feelings are connected with spirituality but they are relative to every other area of your life in this world. Even the clerk at the store who does not even know you is subjected to the attitude caused by your emotions.

We need healthy *fear* to respect God and human authority and to warn us of danger. Fear secretes hormones that give us the power to fight for our lives when necessary and calls us to subjection under authority. However, when fear takes over our life it makes us timid. We need controlled productive *anger* to insight us to take action against injustice. However, when anger takes over it can destroy our lives. We need appropriate *happiness* to enjoy life. However, most adults know someone who is always happily laughing when it is not appropriate, seeming not to know when to take matters seriously. We need a healthy amount of *worry* when engaging in wrong activity. If we can commit wrong with pure boldness then we will not be prompted to take precautions about the outcome of behavior. The EFT can help tune emotions to appropriate levels.

Step 2: Along with EFT, I acknowledged that I did need the power of God to help repair my damaged spirit and help to correct the destructive behavior of my emotions.

Action: EFT set up phrase:
Even though I let negative thoughts take control of my mind and cause me to live in isolation after _____, I still deeply and completely love and accept myself
MUST BE PERSONALIZED

Step 3: I decided to stop "feeding God with a long handled spoon" and made an effort to take steps to begin fully trusting as I did back when I was a child before the sexual abuse began. Back then I was happy being in Sunday school, praying and working around the church, God's house.

Action: EFT set up phrase:
Even though I was not able to trust God as I did in the past because_____. I still deeply and completely love and accept myself.
MUST BE PERSONALIZED

Step 4: I admitted to God regardless of what occurred in my life I should have remained in his presence and that it was my fault for becoming distant, not his fault for running me away.

Action: EFT phrase:
Even though I was wrong to blame God for _____, I still deeply and completely love and accept myself.
MUST BE PERSONALIZED

Step 5: I admitted that I only attended church out of ritualism.

Action: EFT set up phrase:
Even though I was not sincere when I attended church because _____, I still deeply and completely love and accept myself.
MUST BE PERSONALIZED

Step 6: I confessed that I was ready for a change in my life and in our relationship.

Action: EFT set up phrase:
Even though I became complacent by _____, I still deeply and completely love and accept myself.
MUST BE PERSONALIZED

Step 7: I asked God if he would help me to correct the error of my ways and restore me back to him.

Action: EFT set up phrase:
Even though I made a mistake in our relationship by _____, I still deeply and completely love and accept myself.
MUST BE PERSONALIZED

Step 8: I made of list of the people who needed me and I was unavailable because of wallowing in self-pity.

Action: EFT set up phrase:
Even though I was not available to help when (John, Jane, etcetera) needed me because _____, I still deeply and completely love and accept myself.
MUST BE PERSONALIZED

Step 9: I acknowledged that I would like to make

amends, but judgment is required since there are some people who have become so hurt or angry that an apology will cause the situation to become worse. I would be open if they approached me.

Action: EFT phrase:
Even though I did not make personal apologies to (John, Jane, etcetera) because _____, I still deeply and completely love and accept myself.
MUST BE PERSONALIZED

Step 10: I acknowledged understanding that attempting to go back to my old ways would be a part of the process. It was not reasonable to expect that I would heal and never experience any aches and pains from my wounds at times.

Action: EFT phrase:
Even though I went back to _____, I still deeply and completely love and support myself.
MUST BE PERSONALIZED

Step 11: I asked God to confirm the direction or new direction that he wanted me to take in my life calling.

Action: EFT phrase:
Even though I tried to go in my own direction by _____ instead of listening to God, I still deeply and completely love and support myself.
MUST BE PERSONALIZED

Step 12: I made a decision to renew my life calling.

Action: EFT phrase:
Even though I allowed myself to get off track by_____, I still deeply and completely love and support myself.
MUST BE PERSONALIZED

FOCUS POINTS DURING EFT
The EFT self-therapy is effective because others cannot FEEL your emotional reaction to your unique situation and they cannot evaluate if your feelings are actually shifting. Determine the level of your emotional pain surrounding the issues listed below and use the level of pain to develop set-up phrases. In the past, if some type of statement was made just to pacify your feelings such as:
"God knows what is best."
"You will reap what you sow."
"What goes around comes around."
"One day you will need my help."
"I don't care what you think about me."

If this was said in relation to a situation listed below then there is probably a blockage in that area if you feel an emotional reaction.

❖ YOU ARE NOT ALONE

Whenever someone faces what he or she perceive to be a shameful obstacle or an embarrassing situation in their life, often it seems like they are the only one going through that type of experience.

There are people outside of your family and friends from various organizations who want to help you if you reach out to them. You do not have to live in isolation battling negative feelings alone.

❖ BLAMING THE VICTIM

Some victims do not expose abuse because they fear being blamed for some behavior that caused the abuse or were blamed. Some common responses from adults when abuse is exposed are:

"She/He was old enough to know better."
"She/He was grown enough to go out and do what they wanted to do."
"She/He wanted to be grown."

You did not have the mental maturity to be held responsible for engaging in activities that caused you harm. You are NOT responsible for what happened. The adult was responsible and obligated to remain within appropriate boundaries.

❖ SHAME

The abuse is not a reflection on you; it is a reflection on the abuser. The adult engaged in shameful behavior and they should be ashamed of getting you involved.

❖ GUILT

An adult used their mental wisdom over you to encourage you to do things they knew were wrong. It was not wrong for you to comply with someone who you knew and trusted. The adult was guilty of entrapping you in their deceitful plan.

❖ SELF-BLAME

An obvious factor in self-blame is that hindsight allows you to see things you might have been able to do to avoid the horrible experience, but only the abuser knew where it was leading. It was only afterward that you were able to see how disgraceful the abuser behaved. You were caught off guard and it is not your fault that when things escalated you did not know the correct action to take

❖ FEAR

One of the greatest obstacles survivors of sexual abuse can face is the amount of denial they experience from perpetrators and even loved ones who doubt their experience could have happened. A lack of support can make it difficult to want to heal fully. Some victims believe that if they recover then it will appear that the abuse did not actually occur or that is was not severe so their pain will never be acknowledged by anyone.

❖ ACCEPTING

Although, there was not even the slightest force or threat of harm used against you in a series of sexual occurrences and you were only verbally coerced, what happened to you did involve acts that are defined as sexual abuse. While tapping through EFT in private the healing treatment was only effective when I said specific names or specific situations. Saying general statements for healing related to abuse will be insufficient.

One example of a survivor set up phrase:

Cannot just say: "Even though my cousin did not help me when I needed her, I still…"

Instead would say: "Even though I feel anger and resentment when I think about the time I told my cousin Jane Doe that her husband John Doe touched me and she said I should not have been trying to act grown, that made me feel she valued having a relationship with a man more than she valued my pain. I still…" (or whatever is relevant to your situation)

Often, a victim/survivor will make statements such as:

"My family wasn't there for me."
"My mother did not help me."
"My grandmother blamed me."
"My father did not want to be bothered."

These type of statements used as set up phrases will not lead to successful EFT. The victim/survivor must be ready to honestly acknowledge the specific situations that caused their emotional trauma and work through why they have a difficult time releasing the pain. Some reasons might be:

* Feel they cannot receive justice until the abuser is punished or suffers pain for their actions

* Determined to hold on to their pain so God will acknowledge the level of trauma it has caused them and execute vengeance on their abuser.

There are a number of various reason that victims/survivors hold on to their pain. We are all aware that many innocent people have been convicted and even executed. In turn, many guilty people have escaped conviction and walk free. Therefore, it is vital to accept the fact that there is a possibility that our abuser may somehow escape being held accountable during this lifetime.

After a reasonable amount of effort has been made without results, decide to move past your situation and contribute to helping someone else. If you allow your entire life to become consumed with one issue then it will destroy your entire life, which is giving the abuser even more power over you.

I am thankful the effects from abuse led me to seek healing beyond traditional denominational boundaries. The EFT routine helped me to stay focused on my prayer while I transformed from being paralyzed in life because of my childhood experiences to learning how to thrive rather than just survive. I have known a number of Christians who suffered from spiritual depression after preachers and other saints made them feel spiritually inadequate because they could not simply speak a word and cause God to make the sun stop shining for days. This is not an alternative to prayer; it is a tool that helped to evaluate the level of emotional pain I felt, which verified if I was actually healing or just suppressing my feelings over assuming guilt for situations that I could not have realistically controlled physically or mentally.

When prayers seemed to be blocked, the continued EFT therapy assisted in identifying the very specific area of the blockage. Even while saying thank you to God, it helped to evaluate the level of sincerity as opposed to just giving gratitude as one of the routine closing statements to prayer.

Many victims/survivors are uncomfortable discussing abuse with others. EFT was the type of therapy that allowed me to strengthen myself in private; then I became strong in public. I received relief from emotional pain and a shift in emotional balance after the EFT induced my body to restore balance back to its energy system after confronting the blockage and tapping a clearance. Moving from constant self-judgment to self-evaluation, I developed the ability to learn various lessons intellectually while discarding the actual event from my heart.

The tears I cry today are not from hurtful destructive pain. Now I cry tears of joy from purposeful pain. When I speak, the tremor in my voice is my spirit reminding me that it is he speaking through me to fulfill my purpose in life. I have moved from struggling with the grief of pain to living with the gift of pain.

Survivor's Profile In This Story

* African-American female fifty years old

* Inappropriate behavior by abuser leading to the sexual abuse began at eleven years old

* The abuser was a clergy friend to the family through church association

* African-American abuser, Church and Denominational association

* The age survivor believes the abuse ceased to be a destructive experience was forty-two years old

FAMILY HISTORY
* Two-parent working suburban middle class family
* No siblings
* Regular church attendance/ Christian beliefs

EDUCATION HISTORY
* High school graduate
* College graduate

RELATIONSHIP HISTORY
* Married at eighteen years old
* Divorced at twenty-two years old
* No children
* Firm heterosexual — never experienced any sexuality identity issues
* No other occurrences of sexual victimization

Tiffany Denmark

Clergy Sexual Abuse Websites

www.reportcogicabuse.com

www.spiritualabuse.com

www.stopbaptistpredators.org

www.adultsabusedbyclergy.org

www.thehopeofsurvivors.com

www.tamarsvoice.org

www.stopitnow.org

Child Sexual Abuse Websites

www.darkness2light.org

www.stopcsa.org

www.childmolestationprevention.org

www.advocatesforyouth.org

www.malesurvivor.org

National U.S. Sexual Assault Hotline 1-800-656-HOPE (4673)

www.rainn.org
(They will connect you with local assistance in your area)

Illinois Coalition Against Sexual Assault (ICASA) www.icasa.org

Canada Canadian Association of Sexual Assault Center

Vancouver, British Columbia

604-876-2622 (p)

604-876-8450 (f)

United Kingdom Rape Crisis Line

0808 802 9999

References

"Chaplain." *U.S. Department of Veterans Affairs*. N.p., n.d. Web. 30 July 2013. <http://va.gov/>.

"Christian Church Directory : USA Churches." Christian Church Directory : USA Churches. N.p., n.d. Web. 29 July 2013. <http://www.usachurches.org/>.

Church D, Books A. (2010). Application of Emotional Freedom Techniques. Integrative Medicine: A Clinician's Journal, Aug/Sep, 46-48.

"Church Denominations." Encyclopedia Britannica Online. Encyclopedia Britannica, n.d. Web. 29 July 2013. <http://www.britannica.com/>.

"Crime Codes." PAMeganSlaw.com: The Leading PA Megan Slaw Site on the Net. N.p., n.d. Web. 29 July 2013. <http://www.pameganslaw.com/>.

"Fear." Self Improvement from SelfGrowth.com. N.p., n.d. Web. 29 July 2013. <http://www.selfgrowth.com/>.

Feinstein, D. (2010). Rapid Treatment of PTSD: Why Psychological Exposure with Acupoint Tapping May Be Effective. Psychotherapy: Theory, Research, Practice, Training, 47(3), 385-402.

"Illinois Coalition Against Sexual Assault: English: Home." Illinois Coalition Against Sexual Assault: English: Home. N.p., n.d. Web. 29 July 2013. <http://icasa.org/>.

"Introduction to Emotional Freedom Techniques." The Dr. Oz Show. N.p., n.d. Web. 29 July 2013. <http://www.doctoroz.com/

Merriam-Webster. Merriam-Webster, n.d. Web. 29 July 2013. <http://www.merriam-webster.com/>.

"New International Version." BibleGateway.com: A Searchable Online Bible in over 100 Versions and 50 Languages. N.p., n.d. Web. 29 July 2013. <http://www.biblegateway.com/>.

"Personality Disorders." Mayo Clinic. Mayo Foundation for Medical Education and Research, n.d. Web. 29 July 2013. <http://www.mayoclinic.com/>.

" RAINN | Rape, Abuse and Incest National Network | RAINN: The Nation's Largest Anti-sexual Assault Organization.One of "America's 100 Best Charities" -Worth Magazine. N.p., n.d. Web. 29 July 2013. <http://rainn.org/>.

"Relief Fund for Sexual Assault Victims/sexual Assault Chart." Relief Fund for Sexual Assault Victims. N.p., n.d. Web. 29 July 2013. http://relieffundforsexualassaultvictims.org/

"Sex Abuse/self Blame." Bible Christian Help. Jesus Christianity. Support & Encouragement. N.p., n.d. Web. 29 July 2013. <http://www.netburst.net/>.

[2] "Vatican Crimes: Evangelical Pastor Convinced Followers His Penis Contained HOLY MILK, Arrested." Breaking News | Today's Top News Stories: Vatican Crimes: Evangelical Pastor Convinced Followers His Penis Contained HOLY MILK, Arrested. N.p., n.d. Web. 28 Jan. 2013. <http://www.topworldheadlines.com/2013/01/vatican-crimes-evangelical-pastor.html>.

[1] "Victims of sexual abuse by priests share shocking stories" published in The Final Call Newspaper, Chicago, Illinois December 8, 2009 Ashahed M. Muhammad, Asst. Editor

Waite W, Holder M. (2003). Assessment of the Emotional Freedom Technique: An Alternative Treatment for Fear. The Scientific Review of Mental Health Practice (2) 1

"What Is Child Sex Abuse." American Humane Association | Home. N.p., n.d. Web. 29 July 2013. <http://www.americanhumane.org/>.

GENERAL DISCUSSION POINTS

* **Proper use of Forgiveness:**

    Controlled forgiveness with conditions

    Emotional forgiveness without conditions (often induced from spiritual guilt)

* **Proper use of:**

    Spiritual Governance in life

    Legal Governance in life

Tiffany Denmark

GENERAL DISCUSSION NOTES:

GENERAL DISCUSSION NOTES:

Tiffany Denmark

GENERAL DISCUSSION NOTES:

GENERAL DISCUSSION NOTES:

Tiffany Denmark

GENERAL DISCUSSION NOTES:

PSYCHOLOGY/SOCIOLOGY DISCUSSION POINTS

* Different emotional effects with clergy sexual abuse verses family molestation, assault by strangers, etc.

* Difference between silence, privacy and secrecy

* Methods used to shame victim

* Methods used to lure victim

* Post trauma effects

Tiffany Denmark

PSYCHOLOGY NOTES:

PSYCHOLOGY NOTES:

Tiffany Denmark

PSYCHOLOGY NOTES:

PSYCHOLOGY NOTES:

Tiffany Denmark

PSYCHOLOGY NOTES:

SOCIOLOGY NOTES:

Tiffany Denmark

SOCIOLOGY NOTES:

SOCIOLOGY NOTES:

Tiffany Denmark

SOCIOLOGY NOTES:

SOCIOLOGY NOTES:

Tiffany Denmark

RELIGIOUS DISCUSSION POINTS

* Clergy brotherhood code of silence

* Violations of ministerial ethics

* Abuse of power

* Spiritual abuse

* Betrayal of trust

* Church politics

RELIGIOUS DISCUSSION NOTES:

Tiffany Denmark

RELIGIOUS DISCUSSION NOTES:

RELIGIOUS DISCUSSION NOTES:

Tiffany Denmark

RELIGIOUS DISCUSSION NOTES:

RELIGIOUS DISCUSSION NOTES:

Tiffany Denmark

RELIGIOUS DISCUSSION NOTES:

RELIGIOUS DISCUSSION NOTES:

Tiffany Denmark

LEGAL DISCUSSION POINTS

* Violation of public trust

* Violation of public safety (child safety)

* Church liability (in-state and out-of-state)

* Criminal or civil evidence useful for other abuse cases

* Criminal or civil violations other than child sexual abuse

* Litigation limitations for religious institutions versus schools and other organizations where state regulation establishes minimum standards for employees that have direct contact with children

LEGAL DISCUSSION NOTES:

Tiffany Denmark

LEGAL DISCUSSION NOTES:

LEGAL DISCUSSION NOTES:

Tiffany Denmark

LEGAL DISCUSSION NOTES:

LEGAL DISCUSSION NOTES:

Tiffany Denmark

LEGAL DISCUSSION NOTES:

LEGAL DISCUSSION NOTES:

ALTERNATIVE THERAPY DISCUSSION POINTS

* EFT assisted with resolving or decreasing:

Hopelessness

Resentment

Depression

Anger

Fear

ALTERNATIVE THERAPY NOTES:

Tiffany Denmark

ALTERNATIVE THERAPY NOTES:

ALTERNATIVE THERAPY NOTES:

Tiffany Denmark

ALTERNATIVE THERAPY NOTES:

ALTERNATIVE THERAPY NOTES:

www.ingramcontent.com/pod-product-compliance
Lightning Source LLC
Chambersburg PA
CBHW070944100426
42738CB00010BA/2126

Praise for *Scars*

"A unique series for children, by children."
-*Booklist*

"*Scars* makes a fun ride out of the serious topic of peer pressure and offers a fascinating look into the repercussions of choosing poorly."
-Jonathan Smith, Youth Motivational Speaker, I Think School Assemblies

"*Scars* is an easy to read book demonstrating the internal conflict experienced by a person feeling pressured to 'conform' by making a decision just to go along with the group even though he believed the decision was a bad one. There are some decisions we make where we don't get second chances and though we may be forgiven, we can never undo what's been done. *Scars* confronts these issues in a very genuine, well written story."
-Dr. Lewis Ribner, Clinical Psychologist

"A useful resource for school-aged children dealing with peer pressure or bullying. It addresses both emotional and physical scars that may occur during one's school years and beyond. As a result of yielding to peer pressure, it magnifies the importance of doing the right thing and following one's heart in the face of adversity."
- Kim Hogelucht, Professor, Point Loma Nazarene University

"Everyone struggles with peer pressure to conform to the ideas, actions and speech of others. As a current middle school teacher, I look for books that tackle the issues my students are experiencing since very often peer pressure robs them of their ability to make their own decisions. The book *Scars* tells the story of a young boy who was influenced by his friends and later in his life comes face to face with the results of his choices. I highly recommend this book along with the additional resources in the book to engage students in the discussion of peer pressure."
- Jan Menconi, Educator and school administrator